AF335425

To Tell the Story

Poems
of the Holocaust
by
Yala Korwin

HOLOCAUST LIBRARY
New York, NY

Copyright © 1987 by Yala Korwin

Library of Congress Catalog Card No. 87-80791

ISBN: 0-89604-090-9 (Cloth)
       0-89604-091-7 (Softcover)

Cover Design by Yala Korwin
Back Cover Photo by Gaston Dubois
Printed in the United States

For All Those I Love

TABLE OF CONTENTS

ILLUSTRATIONS
By Yala Korwin

PREFACE

Away from home for a few weeks when seven years old, I was encouraged to write a letter to my mother. I drew a woman holding a dog on a leash, and scribbled: "Today I saw a lady with a dog." This account of an event that impressed me so much that I needed to share it was lost, years later, during the war, with other treasured family memorabilia. When I was ten or eleven, I wrote and illustrated a play about some improbable adventures of a book. I wanted it to be performed in my school during the Week-Of-The-Book period, but was too shy to show it to the teacher or to anybody else. I don't know how and where this very first manuscript of mine disappeared, but I went on writing stories and drawing all through my school years.

When, in 1939, the Russians occupied the eastern part of Poland, including the city of Lwów where I was born and raised, I enrolled with great enthusiasm in an art school. It became a tuition-free institution, and, as a good student, I was also granted a monthly scholarship. With youthful carelessness, busy with my studies and my friendships, I paid little attention to the bleakness around me. Father, a Hebrew scholar, writer, teacher and active Zionist had to camouflage his past. Mother lost her job in a family-owned photo studio which became the property of the state. Refugees from the west kept spreading news about the mistreatment of Jews by the Nazis. But the outbreak of the Soviet-German war in 1941 forced me to face reality. Under German rule our lives changed radically. Our former identities lost all meaning. Interests, talents, education, professions, ambitions, didn't count anymore. We became nobodies. All our energies were spent on the struggle for mere survival. A roof over our heads, crumbs of bread in our stomachs, one more day of living. The city became a forest where hunters roamed. We were their prey.

To break us morally and economically, the Nazis kept

changing the borders of the ghetto, thus forcing us to move from place to place. My family rebelled. Disobeying the latest orders, we went back to the forbidden part of the city where we attempted to live clandestinely and precariously until we were denounced. My parents and, a few weeks later, my older sister, were forced into the unknown. My younger sister and I escaped their fate.

I survived the remaining years of the war thanks to a pair of decent Christians, a brother and sister, who provided forged "aryan" papers. Slaving for over three years in a labor camp in the heart of Germany, I had to forget who I was, who my parents were, where I was from. I had to guard my speech, my manners, even my facial expression, and had to review every night the invented story of my life so I wouldn't forget any detail.

The war ended. With no place to go back to, I let the winds take me to France where I met my future husband. We married, had two children. The urge to write about what happened to my family, friends, schoolmates, teachers, neighbors, strangers, never left me. I carried with me images that kept haunting me, but, busy with raising my little ones, I hardly had time to breathe. Moreover, after so many years out of the country, the Polish tongue didn't seem the right tool anymore. French, though greatly admired, remained a stranger.

We emigrated to the United States in 1956, and in 1965, to further my education, I enrolled in Queens College. Remembering the times when I was not allowed to go back to school, my motto became: "Hitler shall not win over any area of my life." Though always attracted to visual arts and writing, for practical reasons I chose to specialize in library work. A breakthrough came in 1982, the year of the first Gathering of the Survivors in Jerusalem. All the participants were encouraged to bring along tape cassettes with their stories. I decided to write mine, and this is how a crude prototype of the present book came to life. Titled "The Other Side

Of Silence," it remained at Yad Vashem with the archival number 5751. I needed a few more years of apprenticeship until I was ready to produce this work in its present form.

Thus, I am submitting my testimony to "the court of memory." This is what happened to me and my people. This is what human beings are capable of. It must never be forgotten. The seedlings of hate must never be permitted to take root again.

Yala Korwin
New York City, 1987

ACKNOWLEDGEMENTS

I owe my gratitude to Mark Cohen, the Executive Director of the Holocaust Library, for his firm conviction that my manuscript should become a book. I am indebted to the members of the Poetry Society of America Peer Workshop, Women Poets of New York and Fresh Meadows Poets for having helped me shape up some of my poems. I especially treasure the valuable critique and advice of a fine poet and friend, Rhina P. Espaillat. My sincere thanks go to *Martrydom And Resistance, Midstream* and *Bitterroot* for their previous publication of the following poems: "When We Are Gone," "The Little Boy With His Hands Up," "Day Of Remembrance," "Passover Night 1942," and "Józek's Fedora," and to Charles Fishman for the inclusion of two of my poems in his anthology: *Blood To Remember; American Poets On The Holocaust*. My husband Paul has my deep appreciation for his understanding and moral support of my creative endeavor.

I.

Pull of Shadows

"The above Jews whom we have reserved for ourselves and the country and for our special treasury may realize during our happy reign that they have found comfort with us."
Boleslav the Pious (1247-79)
Charter of 1264

"The Constitution of 1921 declared all citizens equal and forbade discrimination of any kind. Like so many other Polish declarations, it was utterly unrealized."
H. M. Rabinowitz

PULL OF SHADOWS

I would rather dwell
on bright surfaces, shapes

rejoice in yellow, purple
of daisies and violets

marvel at delicate tints
of mushrooms, eggshells

delight, brush in hand
in wholesome blush of apples

follow green deltas
of cabbage-head veins

relish the peasant-brown
of bread on air-blue ground

but shadows draw me
into the mist of greys

and whispers echo
remember   remember

39 CASIMIR-THE-GREAT STREET

1. *The Courtyard*

The image of my childhood paled
like the old photos Mother kept
in her chest of drawers.
The image of our courtyard grew faint,
but never quite vanished.

Cobblestone-heads scampered round
an old chestnut tree spreading
its deep, refreshing shadows
where I and my friend Jancia
played games of hide-and-seek
and a bridge falling down.

When we grew tired, we just sat
and watched the flocks of clouds
blown helter-skelter across the sky
framed by outlines of chimneys.
The air was balmy, the sun stood high,
laughter glowed in our eyes.

My peasant nanny and my friend's mother
came down to fetch us for our midday meal.
They stopped to chatter. "Look at them,"
the neighbor said pointing at us,
"Next to that damned Jewish brat,
Mine is a darling lamb.

Her skin milk-white, her eyes two cornflowers,
hair like palest wheat in the fields,"

Too young to comprehend, numb I stood,
sparks of gold in my hair, fair was my skin,
my eyes blue, pretty my dress,
and Mama said she loved me.

2. *The Street*

Dressed in cotton with printed flowers,
I waited impatiently in our yard
for Mom and Dad to take me along
for a visit with the auntie.
The landlord's servant, Olga, arrived.
"Look who's here! Come with me, dolly,
I'll buy you a candy."
She took my hand and out we ventured.
The candy she got me was long, thin,
with white and pink stripes.

In front of our house stood Mom and Dad
surrounded by a crowd of people.
"Our little girl is lost," wailed Mom.
Dad said nothing, just stood very pale.
The crowd was silent. Then, they saw us.
Mom quickly grabbed me and held tight.
Olga escaped into the dark hall
as fast as she could, without a word.
Dad said only: "Thank God. Let's go."

"Good people, stop them," a fat man shouted,
"don't let them take her, she's mine!
See how fair she is! Her eyes are blue!
She can't belong to these Jews!"
The crowd grew restless.
"They'll slay the poor child and use
her innocent blood in matzos

for Passover, their damned feast!"
"Save her, good people!"
The crowd began to threaten.

Police appeared. "What's all this about?
Why screams? Why that commotion?"
The fat man turned away in a blink
and disappeared in the midst of the crowd.
The crowd dispersed. We went home.

WITH WORDS AND GLANCES

People who believe in absurdities are in danger
of committing atrocities.
—Voltaire

It began early,
rooted in a young brain,
hurt like a sore.
It began with words
of open haters,
with glances
of false friends.
It began long before
they told me
I was guilty
of killing a god,
long before I knew
that my Sabbath
was not like theirs.

I walked head high
among open haters
and false friends
until the day when
spite was not enough:
They needed more.
They wanted my blood
for they were told
it was not like theirs.

In memory of Leon Reich

A PRELUDE

He was handsome, dark, strong, proud,
    Father's friend.
His voice resounded like vibrant music
    In our ears.
Words flew lively, freely, from his lips,
    Teacher's lips.
Sparks of stars reflected in his eyes,
    Poet's eyes.
He often went hungry and was cold,
    Father's friend.
His coat was shabby, he was very poor,
    Had no job.
No Jew could teach the Polish tongue,
    The poet's dream,
But this was what he knew, what he loved,
    Father's friend.
There was no place to give him chance,
    To let live
This obscure, joblesss Jewish teacher,
    Polish poet.
There was some hope for him, so he thought,
    Father's friend,
With commies or some kind of anarchists.
    Soon he joined.
I really don't know which party it was,
    Father said.
His friend disappeared from our life
    Without a trace.

An infirm beggar on a pavement sat
        In our street.
Eyes of a madman, rickety hands,
        A ghastly sight.
This is my friend in prison ruined,
        Father wept.
Is this what man can do to another?
        I was stunned.
I didn't know what lay ahead —that it was
        Just a prelude.

II.

Ungraven Headstones

"The Poles, except for an honourable minority, witnessed the elimination of the Jews with a serenity approaching the sublime."
Pierre Joffroy

"The United States, once the haven of refuge for the oppressed peoples of Europe, has been almost as inaccessible as Tibet."
David S. Wyman

UNGRAVEN HEADSTONES

Recalled by gestures, glances,
silences, words,
or sudden appearance
of a stranger in a crowd,
they tend toward me
their arms branded
with multidigitate numbers,
torment me with questions,
with demands.

Chosen to survive,
why are you silent?
What have you done
so we wouldn't die
again and forever?
The hour is late.
Wake up, go on.
Carry your burden
of remembering,
of reminding.

Guardian of a handful
of orphaned names,
I inscribe them in poems
one by one.
Before midnight strikes,
I summon my ghosts
to the unveiling
of ungraven headstones.

FATHER

Your last words
to me:

If my name was Ivan
or Vassily
I could go away
far from here
wherever my feet
would carry me

You couldn't go
you were bound to stay
waiting
for your execution

You didn't look
like Ivan or Vassily
you looked
like a man named Jesus
about to be crucified

In memory of Johanna Meisels

HER HAIR WAS GREY

Before I left her
she implored

Don't do anything
foolish, child

Times are foolish
I thought

Your hair is grey
I said

With your hat on
they may spare you

Mother

NOEMI

You hid behind a borrowed name,
bleached your raven crown,
but there was no dye
to cover the pigment of doom
in your eyes.

Night after night I see you
alone in that place
guarded by a killer-fence.
Night after night I am dying
all your deaths.

I didn't follow you, sister.
Can I be ever forgiven
the blueness of my iris,
the paleness of hair — hues of
Slavic fields?

I escaped to be your witness,
to testify: you were.
I live to carve your name
in all the silent stones
of the world.

GRANDMOTHER

I never got to know her
woman-to-woman way.
Her image in young eyes:
a well preserved fossil
of an unstudied species.
Behind her wooden house
a field of yellow flowers.
"Don't pick," she said,
"today is *Shabbes*."
She travelled to the city
with a white enameled pot.
Her daughter-in-law's style
of keeping a kosher home
was not strict enough.

Did she walk so straight
because she learned
to carry sheets of glass,
from, may he rest in peace,
her Nathan, the glazier,
the only in *Cholojów*
and the countryside around?
Widowed, she went on
with Grandfather's trade
to fill the stomachs
of five ungrateful sons.

I do not know her day
of dying, but I imagine
her body inert on a bed
of shattered glass, among
blood-stained buttercups.

In memory of Laura Meisels

AUNT LOLA

September 1939. A sudden air-raid
over a Polish town.
Before running after the others
down to the cellar,
I grabbed a box of wafers.
I distributed justly.
She asked for another,
No, I said
with teenage self-righteousness,
they must be even for everybody.

Dark-eyed, slim, soft-spoken
Her husband left her
and she became a cook-maid-nurse
in Mother's household.

September 1942.
She remained behind,
the janitress told me,
alone in the cellar.
The henchmen who took the others away
didn't notice her meager shape
hiding in a dark corner.

She remained behind
alone in the cellar
without food for two weeks
until a passerby noticed
in a cleft between the pavement
and locked door
a pair of strangely twisted hands
begging.
For bread?
For deliverance?

In memory of Regina and Isidor Gross and their three daughters

OUR THREE COUSINS

Our three cousins
Irena, Gisela, and Malvina
(alias Maria)
changed their faith.
They wore crosses,
dated Christian men.

Opportunism, cowardice,
treason, we said.
Sighed Aunt Regina
and Uncle Isidor:
We couldn't prevent it.
Our girls, at least
may have better lives
in this Polish state.

Our three cousins,
Irena, Gisela, and Malvina
(alias Maria)
went under
with their crosses.

In memory of Klara and Matylda Schrager

MATYLDA'S BLOND TRESSES

Aunt Klara is wary of speeches
by a man with a mustache.
Each day she asks the mailman:
Anything for us?

Her child with blond tresses
is born to become a star
in America. If not, she'll sew
or help in a store.

Aunt Klara combs Matylda's hair:
Good night. Sweet dreams, love.
Our bags are packed. Tomorrow
the visa will arrive.

Matylda's blond tresses
sponge the crimson pavement.
The skin of her body is pale.
Translucent.

*In memory of the three brothers Meiseles: Joseph of France,
Naphtali of Austria, and Gedalia of Poland.*

STRANDED

Stranded in gentile lands,
burdened with names
leading to lineages
of biblical ancestors,
had virtues, frailties.
Prayed, swore,
quarrelled with God,
blesssed and cursed
their chosenness.
Poor — gave to the poor.
Multiplied.
Fought for fatherlands
who will disclaim them.
Had rights — on paper.
Few choices.
Ordinary people.
Not vermin.

*In memory of Paula Królik, Lila Eiszynska, Elżbieta
(Ciuka) Berger, and Elza Eisenberg.*

*Paula sang with lyric soprano; Lila played Chopin on her
mother's piano; Ciuka, a myope albino, painted her world
with hues of a rainbow; Elza was also a potential singer.*

BIRTHDAY PARTY

"Tonight we'll celebrate your birthday,
invite some friends," said Father.
I was shocked. "Here, in the cellar?"
We lived there since the Nazi onslaught.
What a strange idea. An act of defiance?
Premonition this may be the last time
we'll be together?

       They all appeared:
Paula, Lilka, both Elzas, and Ciuka.
With my two sisters, Mother, Father, me,
we were ten celebrants. Mother made us tea,
and Father drew out of a secret cache
a fairly large piece of dark chocolate.
He got it on the black market, he explained
and divided it evenly into ten.
We ate, drank, and were quite merry.
Our guests departed. I thanked my parents.

I never again saw my friend Ciuka.
She went home to join her folks
in a collective suicide.

III.

Jewish Cemetery

*".... at 7 striking, a train of 45 carriages
arrived from Lemberg (Lwòw).* Behind the
barbed-wire openings of the wagons
appeared awfully lean children, and men
and women with terrified faces. Two hundred Ukranians wrested the doors and
whipped the people out of the carriages. At
the arrival of the train 1,450 people out of
6,700 were already dead."
Gerstein's Report

JEWISH CEMETERY

It was part of our lives
like death itself
history
link with the past.
We descended from these
who waited
under the mossy stones
beneath ancient trees
for us to join them
after we lived enough.
We cherished
this final home of ours.

The enemy knew
that in order to destroy
our future
it was imperative
to destroy
the old cemetery
our past
our future past.

TO ANDA ECKER, A POLISH POET

Long time ago,
in the old Jewish cemetery,
near a grave of a friend,
I noticed yours.
Already famous when young.
I read your poems
full of sadness and lost hope.
You killed yourself
for love of a man.
I stood there in awe
admiration and sorrow
for your wasted life.

Your grave is no more.
It succumbed to the blows
of hammers
on specific orders
of a murderer.
You perished twice.

JANOWSKA STREET

Herded onto a hoodless truck,
out through the camp's gate,
they were driven across the town.
No one knew where to. No one asked.
Passersby averted their eyes.
Some crossed themselves discreetly.

Snatched away from their streets
only months, weeks, days ago,
altered from the spirited beings
into lethargic, emaciated shells,
did they know where to?
Ash-grey, shaven heads dangled.

Passersby averted their eyes.
Some crossed themselves discreetly.

BRAVE VOLUNTEERS

Singled out for the job
for youth, boldness, strength,
the brave volunteers
were lured with no way out.

Order and safety must be
preserved among you, Jews,
they were told. What a task!
Order and safety — great words.

Before they knew what t'was about,
they became hangmen's helpers,
indispensable hands.
Some felt trapped, eager others.

Order? First you round up
the old, then children, and young
at the end. In this order.
Safety? Could one speak of it?

Maybe yes. For themselves
and the families. Their own.
Could one believe in safety?
They prefered the delusion.

Bribes? Why not? Food was dear
on the black market. With a bribe
a victim could buy a few more
days or hours of breathing.

Prestigious and often rich
among their own brethren,
in front of the masters
they were little, indeed.

Dependent on fickle whims
of the murderous scum,
they perished in the end
with the rest of the crowd.

In memory of the Girl whose name vanished with her

THEY HAD A SYSTEM

She went to the bakery
just around the corner
to get rations of bread
for them all.
She didn't let her mother go.
She said: stay home.
Yesterday
they took old people away.
Where to?
No one knows.
Stay. I'll go.
She went and didn't return.
That day
they took the young ones away.
They had a system. They were
thorough.

Her mother worried. The girl
had nothing warm on.
Winter was near and winds
were quite strong already.
How will she work in the cold
wherever they had sent her?
Then, a postcard arrived.
Just a few words scribbled
with the girl's hand:
Dear Mama. I'm well.
Work isn't hard.
Don't worry.

Her mother worried.
She put the girl's warm coat
in a box,
made a neat package
and waited.
She waited for another postcard
with an address on it.
It never came.

They had a system.

NIGHTMARE

Eins zwei eins zwei eins
marching boots clatter

on the cobblestones in the dark.
The command stops short: *halt!*

A fury of mad pounding:
Verfluchte Juden raus!!! Raus!!!

Are the violators of the night
at my door? The neighbor's?

It doesn't matter
All doors are one.

Schnell!!! Aufmachen!!!
Alone with my fright.

No place to hide.
Nothing here but my bed

a bare floor
a patch of blacked-out window.

A scream.
The neighbor's.

Mine.

TYPHUS! BEWARE!

A grotesquely distorted
face of a Shylock
invented
with a spiteful brush.

JEWS
CARRY
LICE
proclaimed the posters
all over town.

For weeks
we hid in a cellar.
No time to take off
our shirts.
No water to wash.

We sat
and killed the vermin
with the flame of a candle.
We wept
from disgust.

FATHER'S CHESS

Borders of the ghetto
at last defined:
from this street to that
from this house to that.
Nowhere else.
We could take along
pots and pans
some clothing
nothing else.
But Father said: let's
not forget my chess.

Strangers moved in
gladly and swiftly
to our still warm nest.
We began to settle
somewhere else
when new orders came:
from this street to that
from this house to that
and nowhere else.
Father said: let's
take along my chess.

At the underpass
we were ordered
to open our trunk.
They flung everything
to the ground.

An SS-man barked:
Pick it up! Shove off!
In the snow remained
a king, a queen
and one pawn
of Father's chess.

*In memory of the girl who didn't let her mother go alone,
and the three strangers, mother, father, daughter who
believed in resettlement*

A ROUNDUP

Your work-card? Today
only red stamps are honored.
Mine is blue.

Yours? The girl produces
a piece of paper.
You're free. Your mother goes.

I go where she goes!
The man in the navy-blue uniform
shrugs his shoulders.

Driven by hefty Ukrainians
a band of wretches
clumps through the streets.

We arrive at a schoolhouse.
The room is packed, the air dense.
Complaints, cries.

A family of three
sits calmly on their bags
neatly packed and labeled.

From behind cartons with books
I hear screams, scuffles,
then nothing.

Through the window, floors below,
I see trucks being loaded.
Loud, swaying mass of bodies.

Thrusts of rifle-butts, curses,
then nothing.

*In memory of 16 years old Jerzy Nadel, Irena Milstein,
Stenia who sang for us, and all the others*

THE GIFT OF LIFE

I. *Städtische Werkstätte*

Another *Aktion* ended.
The population of the ghetto
dwindled considerably.
Those who were spared
went on living.
"Jews, rejoice,"
exhorted a Judenrat official,
"this was the last *Aktion*."
He was assured
by a high German authority.
"But you must work
for the glory of the *Reich*."

Workshops were created for
tailors, furriers,
cobblers, hatmakers,
cabinetmakers, turners,
blacksmiths, ironworkers,
electricians, mechanics,
and even milliners.
"What would they need
women's hats for?"
"Don't worry. When a soldier
goes home on a furlough,
he needs a gift for a *Frau*
or a *Liebchen*. Just work."

Great was the zeal of the Jews.
The pay was generous:
the gift of life.
Who wanted more?
One day the Germans came
to stamp all the work-cards
with blue ink. "In case
of a new *Aktion*, you will be
protected," they said.
Next morning hell broke loose
in the ghetto.
They were grabbing
everybody in sight: young,
old, children, and those
with work-cards stamped
with blue ink.

The workshops' chiefs complained.
"Don't worry," they were reassured,
"tell your workers
to stay for the night.
No one should go home
for their own protection."

At midnight trucks arrived
and carried away
the tailors, furriers,
cobblers, hatmakers,
cabinetmakers, turners,
blacksmiths, ironworkers,
electricians, mechanics,
and all the milliners.

II. *The Milliners*

They sat around their tables,
young girls with silken hair,
velvety skins, milky hands,
bred with too much fondness.
Around their tables they sat
handling unyielding straws,
shaping useless wares
with hurting fingers.
The youngest, merely fourteen,
stood at her place and sang
with a lovely alto:

> Great is my love,
> dearest girl,
> impossible to banish
> from my heart.
> It must return one day
> with a song.
> I'll sing it for you.
> You'll blush like a rose
> and when I ask:
> do you love me?
> you'll answer: yes.

They listened quite oblivious
to the present squalor,
they listened enthralled.
"You musn't go home," they were told,
"stay here under vouched protection."
"Another *Aktion* will begin tonight."
They stayed at their tables.
Time dragged. Exhaustion took hold of all.
They begged the young maiden:
"Sing for us your song of love!"
The little one acquiesced, stood up,
then collapsed with a bitter sob:
"*Mama* . . . oh *Mama* . . . *Mama* . . . oh *Mama* . . ."

PASSOVER NIGHT 1942

not a crumb of leavened
or unleavened bread
and no manna fell

no water sprang out
of the bunker's wall
the last potato was gone

we sat and we munched
chunks of potato-peels
more bitter than herbs

we didn't dare to sing
and open the door
for Elijah

we huddled and prayed
while pillars of clouds
massed above our heads

and pillars of fire
loomed like blazing traps

THE UNHEARD BARD

He rhymed, said he, when he was four.
His folks were proud to have a son
with talent, but since the Nazis came,
he stopped writing poems.

He lacked inspiration, he admitted,
in life so hopeless, so drab.
Nothing could move him anymore,
nothing could sadden nor delight.

Until, his parents taken away,
he, suddenly left all alone,
grieving and weeping, felt again
his idle pen catch a new fire.

We judged it monstrous. How could he
exalt when all kept silent?
How could he create when his world
a painful death was expiring?

We were young, quick to condemn,
and saw in him a novel Nero
elated by the flames devouring
his own kin, his own tomorrow.

Today I mourn the youthful poet,
the lonely victim of vile crimes.
The fatal horrors he described
were not of his own making.

His lute and songs became a refuge
left him before he also perished
an unheard bard, nameless shadow.

*For the Italians, friends of the Jews,
stationed in 1942 in Lwów*

SINGING IN THE SUN

Be still as a mouse, warned my gentile friends.
So I sat there, half-holding my breath,
in a dark corner of the hiding place,
an empty garage. Till I heard her sing.

If only I could catch but a glimpse
of her who among such sorrows and pains
can remain so joyful, so spry.
I glued my face to a cleft in the door.

Hanging out her freshly washed linen
on a thick rope stretched across
two trees in her garden,
she was humming a merry, lively tune.

The sun gilded the crown of her hair,
air tinted the skin of her cheeks,
sky brightened the glow in her eyes,
she was free to sing and rejoice.

Piercing envy filled me to the brim
as I moved my face a bit closer,
much too close. Sudden screech of old planks.
Too late to recede. She approached. I froze.

She stood there watchful, anxious, keen.
Let me live, my frightened eyes implored,
don't denounce me. I'm young as you are.
Let me sing a carefree song once more.

Did she notice my dispirited gaze?
Did she guess my silent, ardent prayer?
She just stood there, then she turned away
and slowly went back to her chore.

For Kazimierz and Helena Moździerz
who helped me escape

THE CITY OF SHADOWS

Ancient stronghold of lions,
witness of my youth,
disputed by four tribes,
you grew strong under the kings
who in their wisdom
let my forefathers,
the wandering members
of a mercantile folk,
settle among your princes,
husbandmen and serfs.

Conquered stronghold of lions,
tomb of parched remains
of my torn roots,
I had to leave you
like a thief, at night,
eyes cast down,
for fear of betrayal
by former neighbors,
scions of princes,
husbandmen and serfs.

Pillaged stronghold of lions,
strangers now walk your streets.
I was told,
your splendor is gone.
Long, long I searched
for your medieval charm
in cobblestoned lanes
of foreign towns.
Pavements of concrete
are wide and straight.
They do not lend themselves
to dreams.

IV.

Encounters

Within the context of their campaign of demoralization, the "technicians" had set up a large number of arms factories in the Warsaw ghetto. In order to escape the raids, the Jews had to have work certificates. To obtain these they had to be hired by one of these factories, and thus help their enemies in their war effort. What should they do? . . . they asked Rabbi Isaac Nussenbaum this question. "To live is a Mitzvah, he replied. "When they attacked our souls, we joyously mounted the funeral pyres for the sanctification of the Name. But now that it is our bodies they are after, the time of the sanctification of Life begins."

J.-F. Steiner

ENCOUNTERS

I. *Going West*

She opened her suitcase. I didn't have any.
Mine was a bundle of rags I collected
in a vacant apartment of departed friends.
I had to own luggage for the trip.
I saw her neatly folded garments. She still
had her mother. Mine was gone. Only a mother
could so lovingly put all these pretty things
alongside portions of food. She still had food.
I already devoured my loaf of claylike bread
we all received at the transient camp.
We were a group of twenty going west.
Twenty Polish workers carefully picked.
No Jews among them. None of this vermin.
I fooled the enemy. As to others — could one be sure?
Some of them peasants, most low-class city youths.
Who knows, however? Who could vouch at such times?

She opened her suitcase, took out a sandwich
and a tomato, then at the window she slowly ate
seemingly enjoying the swiftly changing views.
I came and stood beside her. She couldn't fool me.
It was quite obvious she was what I was.
We exchanged platitudes concerning the landscape.
Spoiled brat, I thought judging by her way of nibbling.
When she was little, her mother fed her pleading:
One for me, one for dad, one for grandma.
I watched her eating. Juice of the ripe tomato
drifted down her butter-smeared chin.

51

My empty stomach rebelled, and my saliva
almost choked me. Tomatoes were my favorite fruit.
In a small voice I squeezed in between two praises
of the autumnal vista, blush on my cheeks:
"I would so enjoy a piece of your tomato . . ."
"If I gave it up," she quickly responded,
"what would I eat?" We went on and on talking,
praising the beauty of spacious fields,
somber forests, and limpid hurrying brooks.

II. *Your Train Was Heading East*

It took only seconds for our trains to meet
in the middle of that obscure station
on the borderline between life and death.
My train was going west,
carrying me in a third-class wagon
to live.
Yours was heading east.
I saw your face in the latticed aperture
of the cattle wagon.
Your dark eyes in a tawny face
of a Shulamite
gazed into mine, querying, accusing.
I read a story of a hunted people,
my own people, written in your eyes.
My arms stretched out to you
as I called: sister — only in my mind.
All you could see was my bland stare
and my mouth nonchalantly chewing
a morsel of bread.
How could you know I was not allowed
even a blink of an eye for your sake?
How could you know I also was a prey
of our common foe watching, spying

for a slightest sign
of my semitic descent?
You couldn't know I also was famished
as I was munching my crumb of stale bread,
making it last so one one could guess
it was all I had.

It was midday, and my companions
on that long journey
unpacked their bundles of food.
Maddening aroma of sausage, onions,
cheese, fresh apples,
was reaching my nostrils
filling me with a qualmish sense
of vacuity as I stood there
at the open window.
You couldn't know
I was as frightened as you.
But I still had hope.
Forgive me, sister.
Your tragic, ageless face
will haunt me
till the end of my days.

III.   *Meta-Polte-Werk*

Laughter and carefree small talk mingled
with the tapping of wooden shoes
as the workers marched in pairs or groups
toward the factory. It was still dark.
I was glad my companion kept silent
while we walked following the crowd.
My heart was heavy, much was on my mind.
Sudden blast of wind chased a ragged cloud
away from a disk of a lingering moon.
In its spookish, shimmery glint

I saw the girl's face, eyes full of tears.
"Her sorrows," I thought, "are like my own."

We arrived at a gate bearing a sign:
Meta-Polte-Werk. Our passes checked,
we went in, each to her post, overwhelmed
by the rattling and pounding of gears
and metallic clamor of cartridges
slamping into wooden containers.
A languid *Lied* of the German girls
in a control room, still rings in my ears:

> *Es geht alles vorüber,*
> *Es geht alles vorbei,*
> *Nach jedem Dezember*
> *Kommt wieder ein Mai.*

> Everything comes to pass,
> Everything fleets away,
> After each December
> Will follow new May.

It was late November. Rumors went around
about Stalingrad's valiant defense.
Soon, in January, the proud Teutons
shamefully surrendered. All songs stopped
replaced by constant agitated chats
about husbands, lovers, brothers, lost
perhaps in the snow-covered fields.
But we, in bondage, rejoiced.
Could our freedom be around the corner?
Yet, nothing happened. For two more years
and two more scores of days we toiled,
waited, prayed for the end of the war.
The German *Mädchen* resumed their songs.
Nach jedem December kommt wieder ein Mai
resounded again in the bustling halls.

RAGS

Your machine must be spotless
before you go back to the camp.
Must be shiny
like *Meister* Hase's boots.
He wouldn't suffer
a slovenly slave. *Sauberkeit*
über alles, verstehst?
First, pour out
the slimy liquid soap
heavy with particles of metal,
then rinse with clear water
and wipe with rags.

See that pile of rags?
They come in all colors, shapes.
This one looks like a jacket.
It belonged to a man.
The other was a woman's dress,
and the soft pink wool —
a baby's winter coat.
The piece of blue velvet
embroidered with silver threads
was what they were using
to cover a challah
at their Sabbath table.

MIND YOU, FOREIGN SLAVES

Mind you, foreign slaves,
do not misbehave,
we'll treat you kindly.

Work is light and easy
in our "laboratories".
We'll pay you fitly
with our own *Marken*.
In our stores you can't
get a thing of value.
Goods of our country
are strictly for us.
Fresh air and water,
Ersatzbier sometimes,
isn't it enough?

Mind you, foreign slaves,
do not misbehave,
we'll treat you fairly.

Meal and roof we provide
for your ease and comfort.
What else do you need?
Any crime or trespass
we'll punish severly.
So, mind you, no circus
or movies on Sunday.
If caught on a train
without a special pass,
we'll send you away
to another place.

Mind you, foreign slaves,
do not misbehave.
We'll treat you gently.

You can spend your Sundays
killing the bedbugs.
We provide the stuff.
It's strong. Efficient.
It can also be used
to delouse your heads.
If you wish to couple,
find your own kind.
There are enough of yours
in men and women camps.

Mind you, foreign slaves,
do not misbehave.
We'll treat you justly.

Liebe is not the same
as love. Just remember,
our German fellows
and our *Deutsche Mädchen*
are strictly for us.
For a *Rassenschande*
you'll hang from gallows.
We'll invite your friends,
if they are in need
of more entertainment,
to enjoy the hanging.

Mind you, foreign slaves,
do not misbehave.
We'll treat you well.

JANEK WAS TAKEN AWAY

He was different. He never swore
while he examined a stubborn machine.
He would take a tool out of his box,
and in a flash the problem was gone.

He was handsome, clever, polite,
well liked even by the *Meister*.
But his comrades hated him with lust.
They accused him of being a Jew.

"Impossible! Jews are not like that!"
"They're vile, despicable creatures!"
"We'll prove that he is not."
To his hometown was sent a wire.

In a few weeks Gestapo arrived,
arrested Janek, dragged him out.
I watched it happen, and at noon,
on my way to the dining hall

went to see a friend, tell about Jan.
She looked very pale and small
by her huge machine. Its soaring rattle
drowned all human voices around.

Only she could hear me, but the others
watched nearby spying for signs
of sadness and grief.   So,
with a bright, most cheerful smile

I calmly said: "Janek was taken away."
She, also grinning, held back her tears.

HEADHUNTERS-NAZI-HELPERS

How to describe
the ever-present fear
biting with pitiless edge
into the very core
of our tired brains?

How to depict
the effort to sustain
carefree smirks on our lips
while sadness in our eyes
was giving us away?

How to explain
the unceasing assaults
of cruelty and blindness
and always watchful spite
of the bloodthirsty mob?

How to fathom
why they wouldn't let us be,
why they so desired
to see us going under
hours before the dawn?

How to forget
the pain of sleepless nights,
the torture of vigilant days
and the wishing for death
to give us, finally, peace?

How to forgive?

A LETTER FROM A SLAVE-LABORER
IN GERMANY TO ANOTHER

It was from "Maria"
(my younger sister's
new, "aryan" name):

Dear Friend: I'm fine.
They sent me here,
to *Pommern*.
I live on a farm.
They feed me well.
They say: Eat, eat
Maria. You need
to be strong
to sweep the floors
to wash the linen
to peal the potatoes
to mend the shirts
to weed the garden
to feed the chickens
to tend the swine
to milk the cows
to clean the stable
to reap the wheat
to . . .
My hands are sore
but I'm fine.

UNWRITTEN LETTER FROM
A GERMAN LABOR CAMP

Arnstadt, November 1943

Dear Sister,
today
a girl got a parcel
with bacon n'stuff
wrapped in newspaper
from our town.

I picked it up
from the floor,
climbed up to my bunk,
read an ad:
"photo-retoucher wanted."
Your job.

I know now
you aren't "Stefania"
anymore.
Noemi forever,
farewell

WHY?

Where are they heading
these angry crews
of roaring steel
cutting their way
with hardy breasts
through the bodies of clouds
strewn above our heads?
Why wouldn't they drop
their avenging cargo
also for our sake?
Only drams would suffice
to smash the gory plant,
force the damn chimneys
to stop spitting fire,
make this hell stand still.
Why wouldn't they strike
at least once?
Too small a prey
for such mighty hunters?

APRIL, 1945

Pockets of German resistance.
Whistles of missiles,
bursts of explosions.
Suddenly
all hubbub stops.

Roar of motorcycles.
Excited voices:
The Americans!
The Americans are coming!
We, the slaves, are free!

Young but stern faces.
No attention to cheering,
waving, smiles.
War is a serious business.
They thrust ahead. Eastward.

Return toward evening.
Some carry bodies
of fallen comrades.

VENGEANCE

We'll slap their faces for every insult,
each prohibition, every pound of crates
loaded with metallic venom we carried,
blisters on our hands. For frostbites
on bare feet clad in wooden gear.
For each thrust in our ribs when eyes
wouldn't stay open wide enough
at the machines, during *Nachtschichte*.
For our constant craving for food.
On their side of the dining-hall
the soup was savory, thick, *nicht-wahr*?
For their swelled pride, arrogance,
disdain for us, the subhumans.
For murders, slapping wouldn't be enough.
This we'll leave to another justice.

We went and saw them all in a row,
on a bench, in front of the plant,
waiting to render their devil-accounts
to the victorious power.
We beheld their meek carriage,
hunched shoulders, cast-down eyes.
Herr Hase with all his stooges?
Could they have been our valiant masters?

We didn't soil our hands.

V.

To Tell the Story

*"Of you who are leaving, a few may survive . . .
should you happen to do so, remember everything, remember carefully. Your life will be no
life. You are going to become strangers to your-
selves and to everyone else. The only thing that
matters, that will matter, is the integrity of the
witness. Be witnesses."*

Piotr Rawicz

TO TELL THE STORY

You are saying, Dorka,
that after I coaxed Mama
today
into the "shower room",
the only thing for me to do
was to follow her in?
You are saying that I,
your brother,
am now repulsive to you?
That you would rather be killed
on the spot
than ever be part
of the *Sonderkommando*?
Are you sure?

I don't want to die.
I'm young, and so are you.
We both have some chance.
Mama didn't have any.
All I could do for her
was to ease her last moments
with my lies.
I know that if I survive
I will be haunted forever.
But to choose death
will be to surrender
to the enemy.
This I will not.

Listen to what happened
after Mama was gone:
before me suddenly appeared
a bearded old man.
He looked like a sage.
Could have been a rabbi.
How would I know?
In a low voice he said:
"No need to waste your *spiel*
on me, son. I know all."

Before a Kapo seized him
and pushed him back
into the crowd,
he still had enough time
to whisper into my ear:
"The only *mitzvah*
left to you, son,
is to survive
and tell the story."

HER HANDS

On a damask tablecloth
two silver candleholders

Her white hands
rise in blessing
over a sea of light
then glide slowly down
to enfold her face

Two white wings
burn in a sea of fire

HOME WAS

Home was a cube of light
roofed by four seasons,
Mother's blessing hands,
Father's propping arms.

Home was a box of smells,
a store of childhood sounds,
sisters' cheeks, knees;
cherry wine, mandoline, books.

Home — a cage of silence,
a vault of remembrance,
a stone of mourning,
a shroud of empty sky.

SEPIA RECORD

*"The photo is literally an emanation
of the referent."*
— Roland Barthes

Two living bodies —
one ripe with fullness
of fruit-bearing years,
the other a promise,
dawn without stain —
struck by radiant energy,
darkened a lining
of silver halides.

Two decades later,
behind barbed wires,
what energy stilled them?
Guns? Gas?

A mother, a daughter
became dead guardians
of camp secrets,
protagonists of tales
grimmer than Grimm's.

A proof that they were,
a sepia record:
profile of one
who gave life
to the infant clad
in finespun batiste,
asleep against her breast.

Two paper ghosts
haunt a gilded frame.

MOTHERS DAY

"You shall love . . ." Harangue. Applause.
Here are the candies. Here flowers.
Kisses. Pink cheeks. Smiles.

". . . and forever cherish her memory."
Fragrance of roses
fills the air of the old cemetery.

What shall I do with my red roses?
Let the winds carry them
to the scattered ashes of my mother?

I'll stay in my room, pull down the shades,
turn off the shallow words of the speaker,
light a candle, weep, but not pray.

How can I pray to God
who let the black-uniformed men
kill her?

HOW DID SHE GO?

to be little
to be afraid
to sleep in the dark
to want mother
to tell stories
of angels in paradise
to help me sleep
in the dark

not to be there
when the time came
for her
to sleep in the dark
not to be there
to tell her stories
to help her sleep
in the dark

not to know
to wonder
to wonder forever
when the time came
for her
to sleep in the dark
how did she go?

HE TAUGHT ME

He taught me *alef-beth*
Shema Israel, Mode Ani.
He sang me *Rebbe Alemelech*
Frère Jacques, Volga Volga.
I'll always remember
his prayers, his songs.

He was never too busy
to answer my questions
about stars, volcanoes,
Tower of Babel, Sanscrit,
Ch.N. Bialik, Mark Twain.
I was forever too busy

to ask what he wrote
when he sat at his desk
and wrote   and wrote

Silenced pages
of orphaned manuscripts
littered a pavement

THE LITTLE BOY WITH HIS HANDS UP

Your open palms raised in the air
like two white doves
frame your meager face,
your face contorted with fear,
grown old with knowledge beyond your years.
Not yet ten. Eight? Seven?
Not yet compelled to mark
with a blue star on white badge
your Jewishness.

No need to brand the very young.
They will meekly follow their mothers.

You are standing apart
against the flock of women and their brood
with blank, resigned stares.
All the torments of this harassed crowd
are written on your face.
In your dark eyes — a vision of horror.
You have seen Death already
on the ghetto streets, haven't you?
Do you recognize it in the emblems
of the SS-man facing you with his camera?

Like a lost lamb you are standing
apart and forlorn beholding your own fate.

Where is your mother, little boy?
Is she the woman glancing over her shoulder
at the gunmen by the bunker's entrance?
Is it she who lovingly, though in haste,
buttoned your coat, straightened your cap,
pulled up your socks?
Is it her dreams of you, her dreams
of a future Einstein, a Spinoza,
another Heine or Halévy,
they will murder soon?
Or are you orphaned already?
But, even if you still have a mother,
she won't be allowed to comfort you
in her arms.
Her tired arms loaded with useless bundles
must remain up in submission.

Alone you will march
among other lonely wretches
toward your martyrdom.

Your image will remain with us
and grow and grow
to immense proportions,
to haunt the callous world,
to accuse it, with ever stronger voice,
in the name of the million youngsters
who lie, pitiful rag-dolls,
their eyes forever closed.

JÓZEK'S FEDORA

That morning they sent us
to sort out headgear
in that hut, you know,
near the crematoria.
All sizes, shapes, colors.
Caps, hats, bonnets,
hoods, berets, biggins.
Piles and piles of them.

Near one edge I spotted
my brown fedora
bought in Kraków
four years before
on Grodska Street.
I stared, thinking:
is it possible?
Am I still alive?
It stared back at me
as if in disbelief
that I was still alive.

I said to Mietek:
pinch me, pinch me.
I need to know
if I am still alive.

I WANTED TO LIVE

No one, least all of us, has the right to judge in these
matters. No man can say: "I will never do that."
J.-F. Steiner

That memorable late spring
of the year nineteen hundred and forty five,
brought together by chance encounter
among ruins of a German town,
we walked side by side exchanging
stories of our survival.

He was handsome. Not many were left
of his stature. I admired
the husky torso, firm profile,
keen glance of dark eyes.
He fared rather well for a man
only days away from camps.

"I wanted to live," he confessed.
"I didn't kill. Not a soul.
Strike, yes. I had to.
They picked me for my strength.
Can you understand?"

I kept silent. We parted.
He went his way, I mine.
Many years went by, but
I didn't forget his question
and still am not able to say
either yes, or no.

HE WAS FOURTEEN, I WAS TWELVE

His eyes like raisins
in a dimpled challah
from the family bakery.

His mouth red as fire
burning day and night
in Uncle's bakery oven.

Raised in Verona.
In dreams — my Romeo.
His *palazzo* — the bakery.

My flame never leaped,
thrived quietly, unlike
those in a bakery oven.

Fierce storm approaching,
thunder growing louder,
Uncle gave up his bakery.

He took the boy back
to where oranges grow.
Cold, dark the bakery oven.

Among the living?
Did he find a Juliet?
Does he work in a bakery?

Or, was he forced in-
to a cattle wagon,
branded, starved, burned? In which oven?

MY COUSINS

> . . . some Planning Committee members had
> reservations about marches and other mass-
> action projects, fearing they "might make the
> wrong kind of impression on the non-Jewish
> community."
>
> David S. Wyman

While I was on my way to camps,
my cousins from a distant shore
walked back-slouched, voices low,
white flags in their hands.
They gathered, quarrelled,
agreed with those who claimed
that not much could be done,
went out to lunches.

I endured and sat barefoot
by the graves.
Cousins mailed a pair of shoes
unmatched and used.
When finally I arrived
at their side of the globe,
they came to greet me
only after it was clear
I did not have demands.
They poked and sniffed my wounds,
but when I spoke,
they stopped their ears.
My yarn was much too gory.

They asked: "So many died,
how did you stay alive?"
I heard them whisper: "She must be
from a rather obscure branch,
a perennial greenhorn, quite unfit
to sit and eat with us."

I think, they would have liked
to find me petrified,
a speechless matter,
cellophaned and labeled
with palatable history,
and ready to be stored
on a museum shelf.

LET THEM TALK TO THEIR LIKE

They have gone through much,
remember too much,
brood, recall,
and endlessly talk
shamelessly displaying
their scars.
They are sick.
Have seen hell.
No one comes back
unscathed.

They should leave us
alone,
let us live our lives
in peace.
If they must,
if they harbor such need
to tell their story,
let them talk
to their like.
They will listen.

ANGEL

All that is necessary for the forces of evil to win in
the world is for enough good men to do nothing.
Edmund Burke

Motionless
you hovered
above the ravine

and did nothing
to stop
the execution.

Merely a messenger
obeying
higher orders?

Enough.
You didn't rebel.
I mistrust you.

I have seen
creatures
with angelic faces

tearing infants
to shreds.

VI.

Echoes

"Living among enemies is nothing in comparison to a life spent in an environment of indifference."

Piotr Rawicz

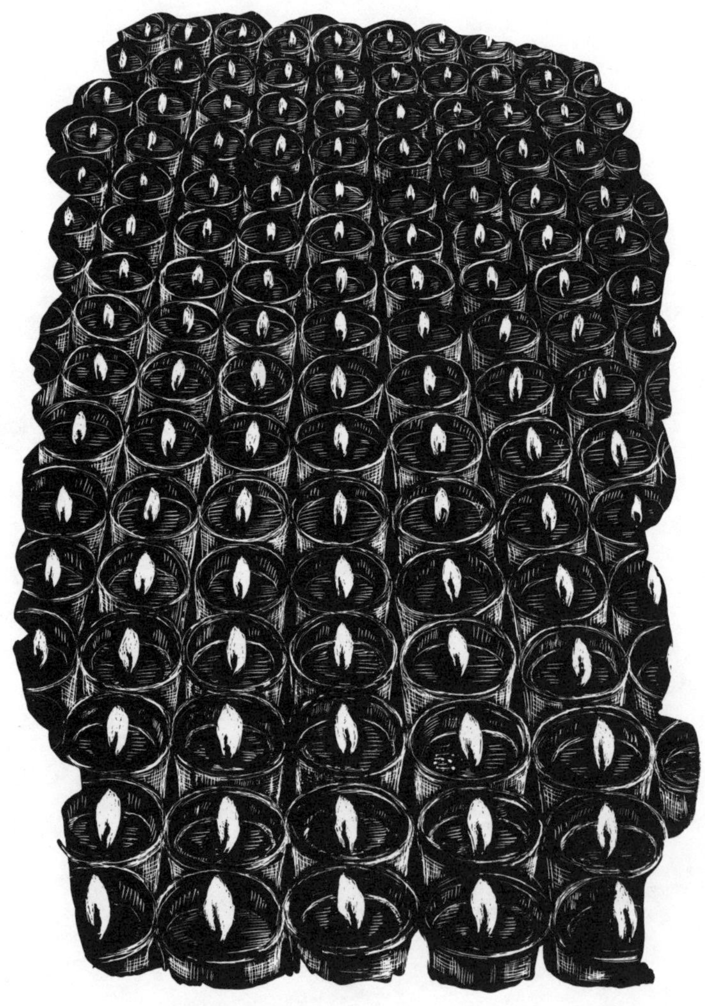

ECHOES

Christmas shoppers
holiday travelers
lights everywhere
eyes bright
crowds everywhere
feet rushing
fingers touching
wares all around
arms carrying
bags all around

a whistle
achtung
stop
wherever you are
whoever you are

trucks arrive
wagons arrive
blacks first
yellow ones next
reds and whites

then all
away you go
where?
nowhere

lights and wares

IN THE FOG OF MY MIRROR

The glass is dimmed.
Outline of a shadow:
Is it me or my sister
Who died in a camp?

You glimpse and gush:
— How ghoulish! Go away! —
In the fog of my mirror
A specter of your face

IN MY HOUSE OF THREE LEVELS
(PANTOUM)

In my house of three levels
The main floor is tidy.
I compose intricate menues,
Wait for the mailman.

The main floor is tidy.
Upstairs I paint watercolors,
Wait for the mailman.
Downstairs I write poems.

Upstairs I paint watercolors,
Apples, roses, and woods.
Downstairs I write poems
Of fires that destroyed

Apples, roses, and woods
I watch somber shadows
Of fires that destroyed
A place with black shutters.

I watch somber shadows,
I muse and recall
A place with black shutters
Of ashes and blood.

I muse and recall,
Compose intricate menues
Of ashes and blood
In my house of three levels.

WE TOLD THEM

Why is our home
empty and quiet
when holidays come?
Where are Grandma,
Grandpa, Cousins,
Uncle, Aunt gone?

We told them
a modern tale
of hellish ovens
and cruel witches
who in new tales
sometimes take over.

Why then didn't
the good people
come to the rescue?
Wouldn't they have won
if all would have come?
Why didn't they?

We told them:
the good ones chose
not to believe
in pits of fire
and those who did
were few and late.

If the world
can be so cold,
if there is wickedness,

if there is hate,
why did you dare
to bring us here?

We told them:
In the darkest night
we carried with us
a tiny flame
that gave us light.
We never let it die.

By miracle rescued,
we brought you here
to bestow upon you,
by miracle born,
this precious gift
to carry on.

WINTER DIARY

On both sides of my street
Denuded oaks and maples,
Chastised prisoners,
Stand, arms heavenward.

Two rows of buildings,
Soldiers at attention
In mud-red uniforms,
Keep guard in bricky order.

My windows cloud and shiver
As winds whoop and whistle
In the smoky chimneys,
In the empty boughs.

In summer, at least,
Displays of greenery
Will subdue and mellow
The coarseness of walls.

Merciful rays of sun
Will wash the bricks with glow
Of ruby and garnet.
In summer, at least

THE PLAINS OF SILENCE

Amaranth-white country of my birth.
Bombers roam over tin-roofed towns.
So many boots marching Prussian style,

So many shadows with bloodless lips,
Lungs choking on the stench of death,
Rotting flesh swelled with maggots.

What did I gain escaping the fate?
I ask myself after the clouds recede.
Alienation. Guilt.

I still surprise myself humming
Old songs of the place where dreams
Of brotherly love were put to rest.

Through fog I see the white eagle,
Crown tarnished, impassively watch
The crashing of stars.

"The world goes well," the teachers lied
And the child believed in lambs and lions
Together in a meadow green with peace,

Beyond threats of dictators and priests,
Under a blue canopy of air and calm
Where lovers and poets invent new words.

Rootless, wind-borne, I still must haunt
The plains of silence, seeking passage
Out of a nightmare.

WHEN WE ARE GONE

The world is waiting
for the last witness
of the great murderous fit
to vanish,
become a legend.
The world is ready
to shake off
vestiges of ashes
from its feet.
The world is eager
to quell
the feelings of guilt,
drown its conscience
in a purifying myth —
catharsis necessary for the mob
lusting for blood.
When we are gone,
the world, able to deny
at last
the reality of Auschwitz,
will shroud the shameful images
from its collective mind.
When we are gone,
the world's gigantic wheels
will go on blindly
grinding,
growing receptive
to the next bloodshed.

DEWEY NUMBER 943.8

Tortured blood
of hardening arteries
in tattooed arms
transfused into pages
will wither

Last witness gone
living words
will petrify
become literature

Dust will entomb
the rows of mementos
on library shelves

A PRAYER

With open wounds in my scorched soul
    that will never heal
        I cannot pray
With heavy smoke of the Auschwitz chimneys
    still choking my throat
        I cannot pray
With frozen image of tortured victims
    in my weary eyes
        I cannot pray
With helpless cries of the dying millions
    ringing in my ears
        I cannot pray
With agonies of the burning children
    alive in my heart
        I cannot pray
With ghostly stench of hollow mass graves
    lingering in my nostrils
        I cannot pray
Because Thou witnessed without sign of Thy wrath
    such unholy deeds
        I will not pray

SURVIVING

Residue of fear
shrivelled down
to the size of a seed
sleeps in the hollow
of my wake

Oblivion creeps in
like a merciful angel
to disband the shadows
obscure memory
alleviate the burden

But I entice back
the choir of ghosts
force them to dwell
in the core of my being
for as long as I live

A GHOST

At a terminal station of a tram
I am standing with one
murdered long ago.

Through some unspoken message
I learn: tickets will not be sold
until more victims come.

One by one they gather and form
a long, silent line. Then,
all are gone. Where to? How?

Alone at a terminal station
I see a wagon arrive.
A huge dark box. Windows broken,

body congested with jagged prongs
of glass. A girl, imprisoned there,
(whose face is it?) beckons me:

Come on! Hurry! Let's go!
I stay and watch the wagon,
grey with the greyest of ashes,

depart. It makes a sudden turn
back toward me. I see it grow.
A shriek: No, Zosia! No!

NIGHTMARE II

Air is dense in the bunker.
Throngs of strangers clad in shrouds
stretch meager arms
above their bony skulls
in obsessive pantomime of prayer.
I am one of them.
Not a sound. Yet,
a tide of exhortations
like an underground river
keeps flooding my awareness:

stay in   stay in   stay in

Precognition of danger
unites us all
like a monstrous dark cloak.
But only part of me does
as others do.
I am also apart, stone-still.
I see as if from a top
of a roofless building
the spiderlike mass of bodies
rambling about the chamber.
I hear warnings:

come back   come back   come back

The danger is out here.
Not a shot is heard,
but I know.
My other self implores:

come back   come back

In vain. There is no way back.
No way back

I LET MYSELF DRIFT

I let myself drift
with a tide of darkness
to atonal space

Swarms of memories
ramble in weightlessness
like bewildered ghosts

Out of reach, far off
words in ant-like stirrings
scour the dust for sounds

On my speechless tongue
pre-taste of non-being
leaves a chill of ice

Till a hint of light
stops the pull of shadows
brings the thaw of clouds

Starts the flow of tunes
triggers a new day-blush
draws a path back home

I let my feet touch
the whirling globe of mud
tinted with fresh dawn

DAY OF REMEMBRANCE

In the court of memory
the case is never closed

through the narrows of conscience
into the chambers lit

with six million candles
the witnesses arrive

their steps — drafts of time
skulls blackened with soot

seeing divorced from eyes
they stare at the flames

and speak with voices
of crystallized silence

as the last candle dies
they retreat

on floors they never walked
footprints of wet clay

on tables they never touched
films of ashes

in air they never breathed
the stench of Zyklon B

the case remains open

SHALOM, JÓZEK

You worried about
your grandsons growing
in a village
of Petah Tikvah.
"In only a few years,
the nine-year-old,
the five-year-old
will carry loaded guns."
Soldiers.

As you were.
But you — will power
was your gun.
Auschwitz roofer, you fell,
broke your bones,
did not surrender.
Jaws clenched, you went on.
No moan. The *fibula*,
the *os calcis* healed.
Badly.

Years passed. You dragged
your lame foot
up the Galilean hills,
across the Negev sands,
from army camp to army camp
connecting artful nets
of power lines.
Light, light to safeguard
a fragile treasure:
Peace.

Now motionless
in a space as tiny
as the one allotted you
in the place
whose memory trailed
along your every path,
your worry lines erased,
old soldier, rest
in peace.

NEVER AGAIN

By the threshold of our days
In silence wait our sorrows

Only once could we prevail
No one survives forever

But the banner-cry born
From the depth of our pain

Shall be a rollling thunder
Over mountains and valleys

Rise with windlike power
Higher than trails of smoke

Drown in waves of anger
Clatter of marching boots

Blessed be the ones who died
Such dying — never again

Such dying
NEVER AGAIN

VII.

Translations

"Among the sixteen Hebraic periodicals were Haoved *("The Worker") 1922,* Tarbut *("Culture"),* Ofikim *("Horizons"),* Kolot *("Voices") 1923-4, and* Tnuatenu *("Our Movement")."*
H. M. Rabinowicz, *The Legacy of Polish Jewry.*

*The two following poems written in
Hebrew, under the pen name "Shalmon",
by my father, editor of a literary magazine*
Tnuatenu, *teacher, student, sage, lover of
music and song, were found by my surviv-
ing sister in Israeli archives.*

*The vignette illuminating "Cupful of
Songs" is a replica of one I made at Father's
request in 1935.*

From *Tnuatenu*, date unknown, by "Shalmon".
(Shlomo N. Meisels, 1887-1942)

KING OF THE KINGS OF THE LAND

King of the kings of the land,
King of wine and of song,
For wine, for a brother I longed,
For a brother who never was.

Come, my brother, let us sit
At the king's opulent table.
There is wine on the table,
Good wine and good song.

Lavish is the king's table.
Servants, pour us some wine.
One cup for me, one for my brother,
And only one song for both.

Rich is the king's table.
Wine is plentiful. Bring us more!
For wine I thirsted and found it;
A brother I wanted, didn't come.

From *Tnuatenu*, Nov/Dec, 1935,
By "Shalmon".

CUPFUL OF SONGS

Mine is a cupful of songs;
Sing me a song,
Strike a golden chord
Of a violin.
A frolicking ray bounces light
To a child of dawn.

The dawn dispatches its beams;
Grab them and rhyme,
Take from a cupful of songs.
Get up, poet, hold on to your loot.
The violin will wake up at night,
The sky will with diamonds shine.

The day is mine,
So is the night.
All is mine:
A violin of gold,
Marvel of a chord,
Cupful of songs.

Page 1 Friedlaender, *The Jews Of Russia And Poland*, p. 32
H.M. Rabinowicz, *The Legacy Of Polish Jewry*, p. 77

Page 7 Voltaire, in Hans Askenazy, *Are We All Nazis?* p. 52

Page 10 Pierre Joffroy, *A Spy For God*, p. 153
David S. Wyman, *The Abandonment Of The Jews*, p. 137

Page 16 *Cholojów*: a small, mostly Jewish town in the pre-war Poland

Page 24 Gerstein's Report, in P. Joffroy, p. 285

Page 33 *Eins zwei . . .:* one two . . .
Verfluchte Juden raus: out, damned Jews
Schnell, aufmachen: hurry, open the door

Page 38 *Städtische Werkstätte:* city workshops
Judenrat: Jewish council
Aktion: action; a euphemism for a roundup of Jews
Reich: empire
Frau: wife
Liebchen: sweetheart

Page 47 Jean-Francois Steiner, *Treblinka*, p. 40

Page 51 *Meta-Polte-Werk:* an ammunition factory in Arnstadt, central Germany

Page 52 *Lied:* song
Mädchen: girl

Page 53 *Meister:* supervisor
Sauberkeit über alles, verstehst?: Cleanliness is the most important. Do you understand?

Page 54 *Marke:* German currency
Ersatzbier: beer substitute

Page 55 *Liebe:* love
Deutsche Mädchen: German girls
Rassenschande: racial disgrace

Page 58 *Pommern:* Pomerania

Page 62 *Nachtschichte:* night shift
Nicht wahr?: isn't it so?
Herr: mister

Page 63 Piotr Rawicz, *Blood From The Sky*, p. 27